CHI

WEEKLY **WR** READER®

EARLY LEARNING LIBRARY

WHY ANIMALS LOOK DIFFERENT

Animal Heads And Necks

Jonatha A. Brown

Reading consultant: Susan Nations, M.Ed., author/literacy coach/
consultant in literacy development
Science and curriculum consultant: Debra Voege, M.A., science
and math curriculum resource teacher

Please visit our web site at: www.garethstevens.com
For a free color catalog describing Weekly Reader® Early Learning Library's list
of high-quality books, call 1-877-445-5824 (USA) or 1-800-387-3178 (Canada).
Weekly Reader® Early Learning Library's fax: (414) 336-0164.

Library of Congress Cataloging-in-Publication Data

Brown, Jonatha A.
  Animal heads and necks / by Jonatha A. Brown.
    p. cm. — (Why animals look different)
  Includes bibliographical references and index.
  ISBN-10: 0-8368-6861-7 – ISBN-13: 978-0-8368-6861-6 (lib. bdg.)
  ISBN-10: 0-8368-6866-8 – ISBN-13: 978-0-8368-6866-1 (softcover)
  1. Head—Juvenile literature. 2. Neck--Juvenile literature. I. Title. II. Series:
Brown, Jonatha A. Why animals look different.
  QL950.5.B76   2006
  573.9'9533—dc22   2006010587

This edition first published in 2007 by
Weekly Reader® Early Learning Library
A Member of the WRC Media Family of Companies
330 West Olive Street, Suite 100
Milwaukee, WI 53212 USA

Editor: Gini Holland
Art direction: Tammy West
Cover design and page layout: Charlie Dahl
Picture research: Diane Laska-Swanke

Picture credits: Cover, title, p. 8 © Joe McDonald/Visuals Unlimited; pp. 4, 5, 6, 14 © Michael H. Francis;
pp. 7, 15, 16 © James P. Rowan; p. 9 © T. J. Rich/naturepl.com; p. 10 © Tony Heald/naturepl.com;
p. 11 © Gertrud & Helmut Denzau/naturepl.com; p. 12 © David Pike/naturepl.com; pp. 13, 19
© Tom and Pat Leeson; p. 17 © Barry Mansell/naturepl.com; p. 18 © Wally Eberhart/Visuals Unlimited;
p. 20 © Ingo Arndt/naturepl.com; p. 21 © Pete Oxford/naturepl.com

Printed in the United States of America

1 2 3 4 5 6 7 8 9 10 09 08 07 06

Table of Contents

Cover and title page: Long necks help giraffes eat leaves on tall trees.

Use Your Head!

Animals use their heads to see and hear. Animals use their heads to smell and eat. They use their necks to turn their heads and reach for food. Animal heads and necks come in different shapes and sizes. A deer's head and neck look different from a coyote's.

A deer uses its long neck to reach leaves and twigs in shrubs and small trees. Its long neck also helps the deer reach plants near the ground.

The deer's long neck helps it reach for plants to eat. Its flat back teeth chew grass and leaves. The coyote's short, strong neck and sharp teeth help it catch **prey.** Each animal's head and neck work for the way that animal lives.

This coyote has caught a mouse. The coyote's sharp teeth can bite through skin, meat, and bone.

This bobcat is ready to pounce. It uses its eyes to tell how far it needs to jump.

Eyes and Ears

Lions and other cats pounce on their prey. If they miss, they can go hungry. These cats have eyes in the front of their heads. Eyes in front help them see how far they need to leap to catch an animal.

Zebras and deer are prey animals. They run from danger. Their eyes are set far apart. This helps them see to the front and sides without turning their heads. This can help them see **predators** in time to run away.

The zebra can see well to the front and to both sides. This helps the zebra see predators.

Birds use their eyes to see predators. Birds also use their eyes to find food. Many birds have large eyes and see well. Owls have even larger eyes than most. These birds hunt in the evening. Their very large eyes can see prey in low light.

This owl is hunting at night. Its large eyes help it see in the dark.

A good sense of hearing can help an animal stay alive. The rabbit has long, cupped ears. Cupped ears catch lots of sound. A rabbit can turn its ears to the front, back, and sides. This lets the rabbit find a predator without turning its head.

This rabbit has one ear turned to each side. This allows the rabbit to hear sounds all around it.

African elephants have very large ears. On hot days, they flap their ears back and forth to cool off.

African elephants have big ears. They can hear far away sounds. Their ears help in other ways, too. Elephants flap their ears to keep flies away. They also fan themselves with their ears to cool off.

When a beaver swims underwater, a flap of skin in each ear closes. This flap keeps the inside of the beaver's ears dry. Camels live in the **desert**. Camels' ears are lined with thick fur. The fur keeps sand out of their ears in the desert.

The camel's ears are lined with thick fur. This fur helps keep desert sand from blowing into the camel's ears.

11

Noses and Mouths

Animals use their noses to smell food. They use their noses to smell their mothers and fathers. They use their noses to smell their babies. They also use their noses to smell their **enemies.** Wolves have big noses. They can smell a deer or a rabbit while it is still far away.

The wolf has a very good sense of smell. It uses its nose to find prey.

An elephant has a long nose called a trunk. The elephant can smell with its trunk. It can also pick tiny berries and lift huge logs with its trunk. It can even suck water up with its trunk and **squirt** it into its mouth.

This Indian elephant is taking a shower. It sucks water into its trunk and squirts it over its back.

Sharp teeth and strong jaws help this red fox chew a hard bone.

Foxes, coyotes, and other predators have sharp teeth. These teeth can tear and chew meat, bone, and skin. Animals that eat green plants have broad, flat back teeth. Deer have broad, flat teeth. Their teeth are good for tearing and crushing leaves, twigs, and bark.

Birds do not have teeth. Birds have beaks. Cardinals have short, strong beaks that can crack seeds open. Hummingbirds have long, slender beaks so they can drink **nectar** from deep inside flowers. Hawks and eagles have heavy beaks that can tear meat.

Hummingbirds need to reach deep inside flowers to find nectar. The bird's long beak works well for this job.

This giraffe is using its long tongue to pick twigs and leaves from a tree.

Giraffes eat tree leaves and prickly twigs. Their tongues are long, skinny, and tough. A giraffe can wrap its tongue around prickly twigs and tear them off without getting stuck by **thorns**. Its tongue also helps crush the thorns as it chews.

Snakes use their tongues to help them smell. They flick their tongues in and out to pick up **scents** in the air. Many snakes have teeth, but poisonous snakes have long, hollow fangs instead. They use them to poison prey and kill enemies.

This snake has two long, hollow fangs. Fangs help the snake grab prey and squirt poison into the prey's body.

Necks

Antelope and deer have long legs. Their long necks let them reach down to eat low-growing plants. Giraffes need their long necks to reach leaves and twigs in the tops of trees.

A long neck helps this pronghorn reach for plants on the ground.

Birds cannot move their eyes so they turn their necks to look around. Flamingos have very long necks that bend in funny ways. They can even turn their heads upside down. This helps them scoop plants off the bottoms of ponds.

Flamingos eat plants that grow in shallow, salty ponds. Their long necks help them reach these plants.

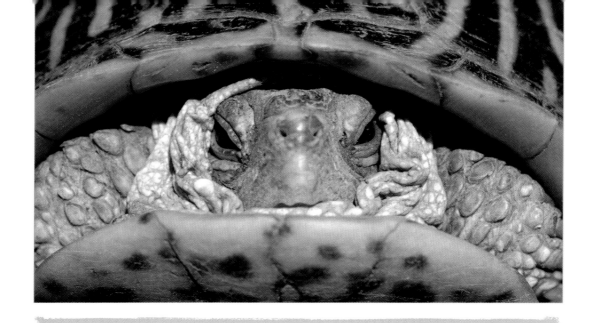

This turtle retracts its head. Now the turtle's soft head and neck are safe inside its hard shell.

Most turtles pull their heads under their shells when they sense danger. Some turtles **retract** their heads by folding their necks down. This move pulls the head into the shell. Others fold their necks to the side to squeeze the head in.

Male frigate birds use their necks to attract mates. These birds have big, bright red pouches on their throats. They puff them up to show off to females!

Animal heads and necks come in many sizes and shapes. Each animal has the head and neck it needs to live.

A male frigate bird puffs up its throat pouch to attract a female. The female has no pouch.

Glossary

desert — land with little or no water, usually hot during the day and sandy

enemies — ones that want to hurt a living thing

nectar — sweet-tasting juice in the center of a flower

predators — animals that hunt other animals for food

prey — animals that are killed for food

retract — pull itself back in or under a cover

scents — smells

squirt — shoot liquid out quickly

thorns — sharp, hard, pointed plant parts that cut and stick animals

For More Information

Books

Animal Senses: How Animals See, Hear, Taste, Smell and Feel. Pamela Hickman. (Kids Can)

Eyes, Ears, and Noses. Look at (series). Rachel Wright. (Franklin Watts)

Tongues and Tails. Head to Tail (series). Theresa Greenaway. (Heinemann Library)

Weapons Animals Wear. Animal Weapons Discovery Library (series). Lynn M. Stone. (Rourke)

Web Sites

Amazing Animal Senses
faculty.washington.edu/chudler/amaze.html
Learn why some animals see, hear, and smell better than people.

Creature Feature: African Elephants
www.nationalgeographic.com/kids/creature_feature/0103/
Read more about these big-eared beasts, and watch a video.

Publisher's note to educators and parents: Our editors have carefully reviewed these Web sites to ensure that they are suitable for children. Many Web sites change frequently, however, and we cannot guarantee that a site's future contents will continue to meet our high standards of quality and educational value. Be advised that children should be closely supervised whenever they access the Internet.

Index

About the Author

Jonatha A. Brown has written many nonfiction books for children. She lives in Phoenix, Arizona, with her husband, Warren, and their two dogs, Sasha and Ava. Jonatha also has two horses, Fleetwood and Freedom. She would have more animals if Warren would only let her! They both enjoy watching coyotes, rabbits, ground squirrels, lizards, and birds in their backyard.